Untangled

FINDING FREEDOM TODAY
AND HOPE FOR TOMORROW

A Devotional Journey

Contents

THANK YOU

As a first time author I have learned many things ...
one being that a book is never birthed alone.

My thanks first of all goes to the team at CWR for their
patience and assistance in making this book a reality.

To the many (too many to name) friends who have
encouraged me over the years in my writing - thank you.

To my siblings and their spouses - Tammi, Werner, Bobby,
and Kimi – thank you for believing in me.

To my dad - Robert Baker - you have inspired me more than
you will ever know. Thank you for your example.

To my Heavenly Father - there are no words. Thank You.

And finally ...

I would like to dedicate this book to my mother -
Barbara Baker.

Observing her daily habit of early morning time with the
Lord is a memory indelibly etched on my mind. Her example
and her prayers have tremendously impacted the woman
I am today.

Thank you, Mom.

I love you.

Introduction

Every day we face distractions to our devotion. We desire to grow closer to the Lord, spend more time in His presence, learn at His feet, and receive from His grace. Yet finding time to nurture this relationship can, at best, be an uphill battle!

This devotional has been designed to assist you in your journey towards greater freedom. Gleaning spiritual application from everyday experiences, each week begins with a devotional on Monday, followed by thought-provoking questions or tasks on Tuesday–Friday – all focused on one main theme each week.

Deliberately crafted for the busy woman, each day should take no more than fifteen minutes to digest. There is also space for further personal reflection so, at the end of the twelve weeks you will not only have developed a habit of regular quiet times, you will also have recorded your own personal journal in this season of your life.

Enjoy. Relax. Be honest. Listen. Receive.

And remember … The best is *yet* to come.

Jen x

Monday

Surprised by Life

FREEDOM FROM REGRET

'In his heart a man plans his course, but the LORD determines his steps.'
(Prov. 16:9)

If life has turned out exactly as you planned, then I am sad for you.

Walking along the seafront of Bexhill-on-Sea, holding a latte and watching the sunset fall against the steady lap of waves, I pondered how life can have other plans.

Most girls do not lie in bed at age fifteen dreaming of life as a forty-one-year-old, never married, single adult; yet that is the hand I have been dealt. It is not out of choice, nor from being too picky (Mr Darcy really does exist, doesn't he?!), not from lack of good qualities or looks (if I say so myself!), and certainly not from lack of praying! Yet no matter how much I planned, desired, prayed for, and looked to have a husband and children at this age, it has not happened.

And I realised, walking along the seafront, there is reason to rejoice in that. If everything I desired in life came to be, how would I know disappointment? And if my goals were met at every juncture, how would I befriend failure? If I kept control of my life, where

would God surprise me? It is in disappointment, failure, and surprise that we are given the opportunity to grow, mature, and risk.

Life lived according to all I desire looks like the ideal life at age fifteen, but at forty (plus!) I recognise *life lived according to my plans is actually a life programmed – not lived.* To fully be alive means embracing disappointment, failure, and surprise – often all at the same time. And when done right, it is the door toward a new outlook, new dreams, all held with open hands to heaven saying to God, *'Fill these as You like ...'*

What needs releasing to Him today? What plan or dream needs to be laid on the altar? He loves you, and He longs to surprise you with a gift you perhaps never would have chosen, but a gift you would not live without. Let Him design the gift for you today.

Who knows? It may even look like Mr Darcy ...!

Spend a few minutes pondering the
questions in the last paragraph about
what in your life needs releasing to God.
I encourage you to write it out on a piece
of paper, put that thing/person/dream
in your hands and hold it up to Him,
symbolising your release of it. Maybe you
are not ready for that yet, but you can
at least ask God to pry open your fingers
a bit and help your heart be open to His
best plan for your life ...

Tuesday

Disappointment is a fact of life. By the end of our first day of life we have already experienced a low level form of disappointment – in the form of hunger pains and dirty nappies, with tears our only remedy for relief! Our desire for life to continue in the warmth of the womb rudely crashed into reality when the cold air of the world first struck our face. Though no child could verbalise it at that moment, certainly there must have been a feeling of loss, confusion, and disappointment that we had suddenly been evicted from our comfortable home into a place which was intriguing at best and terrifying at worst!

Let's pray:

Lord, as I think about areas in life where I have been disappointed I ask that You guard my heart from bitterness and blame. I may not always understand why something has happened, but I trust that You are there in the midst of my pain wanting to bring me once again into a place of peace. So as I explore this area, bring to mind only those things You want me to release to You and help me see Your goodness even amidst my regret and sorrow.

Read Monday's devotional reflection again, asking
the Lord to highlight to you what He wants you
to focus on. Write down your thoughts.

Proverbs 16:9.
How do I deal with disappointment?
Can I embrace failure?
How is God surprising me

What disappointments in life have shaped you
the most?

Lack of good role models.
Lack of direction
Lack of good foundational relationships

What disappointment(s) are you currently
facing?

Loss of relationship.
Lack of reaching or seeing potential.

Wednesday

As we grow older, the disappointment cuts deeper. We learn that promises may be broken, words can hurt, harbouring bitterness is painful, and that our best efforts cannot always stop the inevitable from happening.

And the more often disappointment knocks at our front door, the more we are tempted to ignore the gentle pounding and instead lock ourselves inside – opening that door has proven only too uncertain, scary and painful in the past.

But is locking ourselves inside the right thing to do? Are we avoiding necessary growth by avoiding immediate pain?

Oswald Chambers says: 'If you are up against the question of relinquishing, go through the crisis, relinquish all, and God will make you fit for all that He requires of you.'*

---

* Oswald Chambers, *His Utmost for My Highest* (Grand Rapids: Discovery House Publishers, 1963) p68.

What do you think of the Oswald Chambers
quote and how might it apply to you?

I think that it's the only way to truly see God working to fully
Wholley on his grace, love and mercy.
My situation at the moment
seems very fragile – I need to trust
Wholley on Papa.

Is there anyone you still hold a grudge against because
of how he or she has disappointed you?

Forgiveness is a powerful tool we hold; a tool which
releases us, even more than releasing others. We do not
need to 'feel like' forgiving to forgive. It is an act of the
will. Here is a simple prayer to use:

Father, I choose to forgive *~~Agnes~~ Sandra* for *rejecting me*
I release him/her to Your care and I choose not to be
responsible for the outcome. By an act of my will I choose
to bless them with my actions and words. I repent of
bitterness of heart, envy, anger, and malice and ask that
You purify my own heart in this matter, so I see with Your
eyes and not my natural eyes. I trust You, Lord, to bring
freedom and blessing to both myself and *Agnes/Sandra*
Amen.

Thursday

How does one begin to dream again after life has shattered hope held tightly, yet precariously, within one's heart? What does one *do* with disappointment?

I believe the key is God's goodness. We must know that He is good before we will trust Him; and we must trust Him before we will fully release our dreams back into His capable hands. So the question is: *do you believe God is GOOD?*

Write out at least ten (if not more!) examples of God's goodness in your own life (be creative and go beyond the 'obvious' like food and clothing).

My new church family - SBB.
My relationship with Vall
Parents who love me
flavia.   living in a free country.
Improved health.   my sight
Friends - H, R, S.
Freedom to read my bible.

Using a concordance or www.biblegateway.com write out two to three scriptures which talk about God's goodness (look up the word 'good' and see where it is associated with God).

Ps 16 v 2 - I say of the Lord, 'You are my Lord' apart from you I have no good thing.
Psalm 25 v 8 - Good and upright is the Lord; therefore he instructs sinners in his ways.
Ps 136 v 1 - Give thanks to the Lord for he is good. His love endures forever.

Think about how God might encourage you, kindly, gently and firmly, to begin moving on from this disappointment. If helpful, imagine yourself giving this advice to a good friend – what would you say?

Ask God to help you dream again. Tell Him your fears, and ask Him to plant new dreams and visions in your heart for what He is doing *now*. By letting go of the old, we are then free to embrace the new.

Friday

'**H**is [mercies] … are new every morning'
(Lam. 3:22–23). The sun rises every morning;
numerically the calendar changes every morning.
Morning brings with it a fresh start and a new
perspective.

This morning (or afternoon/evening) breathe in His
new mercies, thank God for new beginnings, and ask
for a perspective which sees through heaven's eyes.

From His perspective nothing is impossible, miracles are as
manna (available daily), and time is never a barrier to vision.

Write out a prayer thanking God for today,
seeking out His perspective, and declaring your
trust in Him to help you navigate through
disappointment into a new place of deliverance.

Papa, thank you that I have no good things
apart from you. Thank you that you
are constant, merciful and faithful.
Please show me your perspective on life.
Show me yourself, give me the mind of
Christ my saviour. Help me to humbly
acknowledge my sin and accept your love
and forgiveness in my life! Please
allow me to walk today in your
ways, Amen. Thank you that you heal
the brokenhearted and the disappointed.
Thank you that you are healing and restoring me. Thank
you. Amen

16

Read Exodus 13:17–14:31. What is God saying to
you through it? Record your thoughts, insights,
encouragement, and challenges from reading
this passage.

God guide the Israelites by day and by night
He never left the people.
Do not be afraid - God + the angel of God
changed position to protect the people. The Lord
will fight for you, [you need only to be still]
[Ex 14 v 14].

Though a situation may not change immediately,
we can. Our choices make all the difference to
the day we have, the week we experience, the
life we live. Declare here that you will begin
making choices which honour and glorify God,
and which believe for His best to be released
into your life – regardless of what is seen in the
natural at the moment. Believe that the best is
YET to come!

Thank you Papa, that you are ever before
me. Give me a heart to follow in your
ways - Thank you that I need not be
afraid - that you will fight for me.
That I can stand firm because of who
you are, I thank you in Jesus Name,
Amen.

Monday

Preaching to the Preacher

FREEDOM FROM FEAR

'And he said: "I tell you the truth, unless you change and become like little children, you will never enter the kingdom of heaven."' (Matt. 18:3)

I had been preaching all weekend, a few times each day, and was consequently exhausted, in the most positive way.

The meeting had finished and now we were preparing to leave the building and have one final night of rest before the conclusion of the conference.

As I turned to leave I saw her father motion for me to join them, saying that his little girl had something to share with me. Becoming shy upon my arrival, she looked down as I knelt to her level. After a few minutes small talk, I asked her if there was something she wanted to say. Quietly, yet with conviction, tears filled her eyes and she said: 'I feel God has asked me to be part of your Prayer Team … may I please pray for you?' Then with great sincerity she added, 'I *promise* I will pray'.

Suddenly I felt as if I were very small and this ten-year- old girl very great. The passion in her voice filled my eyes with tears. I looked at her and said: 'Oh sweetheart, I would love for you to be part of my Prayer Team! In fact ... would you please pray for me now?' And with that she timidly placed her little hand on my shoulder, and, boldness overtaking bashfulness, prayed words to soothe away my weariness and strengthen my spirit.

How often have I avoided commitment based on a sense of not being qualified?

We aim for perfection before involvement, when involvement is what God uses to perfect us.

Next time I am tempted to avoid obedience out of fear, may I remember this young prayer warrior.

And like her, may I gain confidence knowing my Father stands beside me offering assurance, protection and help, as His child bravely steps into the unknown.

Have you ever been convicted by the words of a child? Spend a few minutes pondering the innocence and boldness of children. Why is it they can act and speak without fear at such a young age and what is it which destroys that as we 'mature'? If you could throw off responsibility and fear for a day and be carefree, what would you attempt to do?

Tuesday

*W*e aim for perfection before involvement, when involvement is what God uses to perfect us.

What does this sentence (from Monday's devotional) say to you? Rewrite it in your own words – describing what it means for you where you are today.

It means I want to have everything right no exactly what I'm doing how to do it before I attempt it. Where as God uses the unknown of situation to perfect and change us.

Are there things in the past you have chosen not to do out of fear? Is there anything now you are avoiding, simply because you are afraid of the outcome?

The enemy has used the fear of failure to paralyse most Christians at one time or another. We must remember that just because we have failed at something, it does not make us a failure. Sometimes failing is one of the best things that can happen because it forces us to look to another direction, and often what is found through that door is far greater than what could have been previously. In its most basic form, and without meaning in any way to minimise pain or sound trite, failures or setbacks are simply 'events' in life; events which happened and did not turn out the way you would want them to, or expected them to. Though we cannot always choose these events, and some are indeed very painful, we can choose how we react to them (more about choices later).

Write below a failure or a setback which you feel is still holding you back and which you would like to begin moving on from and/or letting go of. Pray over this and ask the Lord to show you if there is anything you should be doing to deal with or move forward from this event.

....

....

....

....

....

Wednesday

Fear is something we all battle at one time or another in our lives. Often setbacks or failures carry these lingering fears which can affect future events or choices in our lives. It is that unseen reality which holds us back from becoming all that God intends for us to be. It seems to be lurking around each corner of change and hiding beside each declaration of belief – just waiting to cut in and take centre stage. The Word says 'For God did not give us a spirit of timidity, but a spirit of power, of love and of self-discipline' (2 Tim. 1:7).

So if He has not given it to us, why do we struggle so hard to get rid of it?

How would you answer that question above for your life – what areas of fear do you struggle to break free from? Or what areas of fear have you found victory in already?

We struggle to get rid of fear because we don't think we deserve anything else. Don't believe the depth of Gods love and forgiveness and wait for Him to condemn us as unworthy. He never will but our hearts and minds are conditioned by our experience.

Is there anything you would be doing or trying
to do if fear was not involved? Is it something
you feel God would like you to do?

*I'd enjoy living with my whole
heart. To choose to enjoy
every day. Being more open.*

Sometimes the best way to face a fear is simply to
challenge it. Is there one thing you can do today
which might make you nervous, but which you know
is definitely within your ability to do? (eg say 'hi'
to a stranger, smile and say a few words to a shop
assistant, share your testimony with a friend, write a
letter to an old friend, visit your neighbour, apply for a
promotion etc)

Read today's scripture from 2 Timothy again. Ponder the
words and speak the scripture over to yourself several
times, allowing the truth of it to sink deep into your spirit.

Thursday

We often fear what we cannot see, do not understand, or might lose. And if not challenged, this fear will take control over what *could* be and instead write the story of what *will* be. But this need *not* be!

Fear was crucified on the cross with Christ and through the Spirit of God we can now live in peace with God and with ourselves. Peace is a fruit of the Spirit (Gal. 5:22), it is something to search for (Psa. 34:14), and it is a state of wholeness (shalom) not a statement of circumstances. *Peace does not depend on what is happening around me, it depends on who is reigning within me.*

How do you search for peace (Psa. 34:14)? What are some practical ways in your own life by which you could choose peace over panic?

You pesrue it - I can focus on Papa. I can read scripture, I can pray, I can rejoice and look to Papa, seek the Holy Spirit not focus on the problem but the answer. Ask God to change and restore my mind.

26

Do you find yourself letting circumstances and emotions dictate your peace level? If so, repent of that now and declare that you choose to seek peace and pursue it – at all costs.

In this season of your life, what seems to block your peace the most? A situation? A person? A place?

My own buzzing mind. The situation with Sandra. My fear of losing Vall, my whole life circumstance. My fear of the future.

Take about five minutes to simply meditate on and think about peace. Imagine a peaceful scene; put Jesus in that scene and allow yourself to ponder what life at peace would look like for you. What is it that you see?

Peaceful empty beach and a real longing within to be there alone with Jesus.

Friday

Even when we learn to live out of a place of peace, there are still times when fear raises its ugly head to taunt us. Those are the times we must choose which voice will guide us into the next stage of our lives. It is a choice which must be made intentionally – and regularly. But once chosen, it is a choice which lets the carefree, trusting child still living within us take steps forward into the unknown, knowing that a loving Father is there to guard and direct us each step of the way.

Reread Monday's devotional. Imagine your heavenly Father standing by your shoulder protecting, supporting, and encouraging.

Then …

Spend some time dreaming. Don't only write out goals which are achievable; scribe dreams which seem impossible.

Write a book
live with Vall
own my own horse.
Be happy
Enjoy life / Job

Dream of what life would be like without fear.
Imagine doing the impossible task you feel God
has called you to do. What does that look like?

Live in freedom - Speak
life, truth, hope, freedom
into lives.

If you are already living out those dreams, and
fear is a quiet murmur in the corner, pray for those
you know who still struggle in this area. Pray for
their breakthrough, believe for their miracle, and
endeavour to encourage them forward into a life of
peace – not fear.

Write what comes to mind as you consider these
things ...

Sue - healing. - health
Val - healing "
Julie - healing "
Fiona - healing "

Monday

What's in Your Sandwich?

FREEDOM FROM RUTS

'Be joyful in hope, patient in affliction, faithful in prayer.' (Rom. 12:12)

I find it intriguing that affliction is nestled between hope and prayer.

When we are afflicted, that is often all we see. We wake up thinking about it, we go to bed dwelling over it, and most of our conversations somehow gravitate toward whatever hardship we are currently facing. It is understandable. Afflictions are no fun and trials are … well, a trial. I don't know anybody who wakes up in the morning hoping for a day filled with misery.

Yet here in Romans 12 affliction isn't denied or avoided – it is sandwiched between hope and prayer. What is currently weighing heavy on your mind? What issue seems to loiter at the bedside waiting for your eyes to open; resuming its pacing at night, an ominous presence as you drift off to sleep?

I encourage you to reign in that storm of confusion and gently place it between hope in a mighty God and prayer which touches the heart of heaven. There really is no safer place.

Similarly, it is interesting that patience is sandwiched between joy and faithfulness. How difficult it is to maintain joy and faithfulness, when patience is screaming for attention!

Yet, *hope grows in the soil of* joy; *prayer is empowered through the breath of* faithfulness; *affliction is borne on the back of* patience. *Each part is vital in making up the whole.*

Just like a sandwich.

Spend a few minutes meditating on today's key scripture.

Which word is most prominent in your life at the moment? Affliction? Joy? Patience? Faithfulness?

Share with the Lord honestly about where you are at and what you need from Him today – He longs to show Himself faithful and He loves you with a passionate love. Let Him minister His grace into your situation.

Tuesday

W e all have choices. The choice to dwell on what is negative or the choice to embrace what is positive. And the type of fruit we bear will be a direct result of that choice.

When times are difficult the easiest thing to do is crawl into our cave of self-pity, nursing our wounds of despair, waiting for the storm to pass so we can get back to life as we knew it before. What we often fail to realise in that moment is that the difficult times inevitably change the shape of our lives; meaning life may never look the same again. But God has given us a wonderful tool which, when used correctly, can change the future shape of our lives into something even better.

Let's spend this week exploring the choices before us, discovering how we can make life-giving ones TODAY!

Read Monday's devotional again, asking the Lord to highlight to you what He wants you to focus on. Write down what comes to mind, or what you are sensing or feeling.

Be joyful in hope, patient in affliction, faithful in prayer. It seems I'm being given new tools

What is the biggest issue you are facing today;
the one which seems to take up much of your
thinking time/worrying time?

*Situation with Sandra – has
affected all areas of my life .*

Ask God to give you the grace to make wise choices,
the ability to see the right choice to make, and the
strength to release what is not in your power to control.
Here is a sample prayer to help you:

Lord, thank You that You hear me right now, even if I don't
feel You nearby. And thank You that You care more about
my difficulty and fears than I do. I ask that You give me
grace to release to You what is not mine to carry. You do
not ask that I walk in fear or despair and You have said that
I can release my burdens onto Your shoulders instead of
trying to balance them on my own. So I do that now and
I ask You to remove from me the need to find a solution.
I ask You, Holy Spirit, to counsel me in the right way to go
and I trust that You will help me to make the right decisions
at the right time. Finally, I ask for Your joy again. I miss joy,
I need joy, so please restore to me the joy of my salvation
and help me focus on all the good things You have done for
me. I love You my Lord! Amen.

Wednesday

The Bible says 'choose for yourselves this day whom you will serve' (Josh. 24:15); it says we can choose life or death, blessings or curses (Deut. 30:15–19); it says we can choose to follow Jesus or not (Luke 14:27; John 6:66–69). Each of these choices has the ability to breathe life into our everyday situations. *But the choice is ours.*

Nobody can choose our words or our thoughts – only we can. Though a pattern of wrong thinking may have developed over the years, choices of right thinking can replace it.

Take a few minutes to think of your natural leaning – is it towards thinking positively or negatively? What was it like growing up for you – a positive atmosphere in the home or a negative one?

Do you want to change? Be honest. This must be thought through and dealt with before any real change can occur. Don't worry about *how* you will change – do you genuinely want to? Are you willing to surrender some thoughts or attitudes you have held onto, to see change happen?

What keeps you from making right choices?
(habits, environment, things you watch/read/
listen to, etc) What inhibits your desire to
change?

*Fear that its not possible to
have a fulfilled life . Free to
be me and do something I
was created to do.*

Which of these are in your control to change?

*All of them that - I see myself
as God sees me and walk with
Him into the freedom He brings
gives, offers!*

We can only control ourselves, nobody else. Take
some time speaking to the Lord about the choices
you can control, release to Him those people you
cannot control, and spend some time dwelling on the
following verse: 'Finally, brothers, whatever is true,
whatever is noble, whatever is right, whatever is pure,
whatever is lovely, whatever is admirable – if anything
is excellent or praiseworthy – think about such things.'
(Phil. 4:8)

Thursday

One of my greatest ongoing discoveries is that I influence my life; I do not need to accept everything it throws at me. Any situation can look different depending upon the attitude I choose, an outcome can be changed because of my generosity, an offence can be overlooked by the grace God has given me – it is all my choice. So … now it's your turn!

Here are some practical suggestions for you to start making new choices:

Write down five positive things every morning before you leave the house. Write down five things in the evening for which you can be thankful. Begin your day worshipping God for five minutes. This can be in prayer, song, by reading the Bible or sitting in His presence.

Take five minutes before you begin your day praying – quietly, loudly, praying in tongues, reading a prayer – whichever suits you for the season you are in.

Take five minutes each morning to speak life (declaring the Word of God/truth) over your children, spouse, parents, friends, colleagues, situations. (And then find times all throughout the day to continue this practice – be intentional!)

Use the time in the shower to speak blessings over those you know, and to proclaim how good God is – sing His praises aloud!

Memorise Scripture for five minutes each day.

The choices are endless – these are simply suggestions. So now it's your turn – which one of these, or one of your own, would you like to begin with? (Write it down.)

I am going to begin every day, worshipping God for who He is.

Always begin with one choice, and then add in others once that one is established. By trying too many at one time, the momentum will be lost and it will be too difficult to maintain. Typically it takes thirty days of consistent activity to change a habit.

So – take some time doing your first choice! Have fun!

Friday

'Let us fix our eyes on Jesus, the author and perfecter of our faith, who for the joy set before him endured the cross, scorning its shame, and sat down at the right hand of the throne of God. Consider him who endured such opposition from sinful men, so that you will not grow weary and lose heart.' (Heb. 12:2–3)

This verse has so many keys to it:

We must *fix* our eyes on Jesus (not glance periodically).

He *knows* struggle – He has been there, He understands.

He has been *victorious* – therefore we can be!

He *persevered* against the gates of hell – so can we!

Reread Monday's devotional and write down any new insights.

'Be joyful in hope, patient in affliction, faithful in prayer'.
I never saw the hope + prayer connection with affliction. Nor the connection with joy / patience and faithfulness.

Spend time reviewing what you have written this past week, and establishing your new choice.

Reread the verse above – thanking Jesus for what He has done and the example He has set. Ask Him to help you solidify change in your perspective – seeing from His place of freedom, not your place of despair.

Final Thoughts: God is good. He has good plans for you. Regardless of what circumstances say today, His answer is always one of love. Rest in His love for you today – bask in His goodness, receive His grace. His burden is light and His yoke is easy (Matt. 11:30) – transfer your burden onto Him – and rest ...

How do these truths make you feel now?
Write down your own final thoughts.

. . . .

. . . .

. . . .

. . . .

. . . .

Monday

The Tattoo

FREEDOM FROM BLIND SPOTS

'You show that you are a letter from Christ … written not with ink but with the Spirit of the living God, not on tablets of stone but on tablets of human hearts.' (2 Cor. 3:3)

It simply said 'Death'.

Normally when having a haircut, death is far from my
mind; and might I add, this is generally a good thing.
Yet on this occasion as I stood at the counter preparing
to pay, my eye caught an image on the arm of the man
behind the counter.

It was beautifully scripted, written in a lovely colour,
and looked somewhat poetic; yet this fine work of art
boasted only one word – 'DEATH'.

Deftly striking up a conversation, I eluded to the bold
statement hitching a ride on his bicep, commenting
on the unique choice of word to indelibly print on
one's body. Mr. Tattoo laughed and said others had
also questioned his decision, wondering if he had been
depressed when it was done. He assured me he had
not been; also that he was not a masochist, nor did he
have a death wish or any other disorder – he simply
liked the design.

It made me wonder: what unsuitable image imprinted
on my spirit am I tolerating, simply because I like the
design?

Insecurity can look quite attractive when it masquerades as humility, or success can appear rather colourful when the true design is labelled pride. 'Freedom of expression' sometimes hides behind the swirls of laziness, while 'I'm a woman of excellence', if not careful, can subtly add bricks to the idol of perfection.

We are lured in by what looks attractive and acceptable outwardly, bypassing the true writing on the wall. Or in this case – arm.

Jesus bore the marks of death all over His body, so we would not have to. Those marks contained no façade – they declared total surrender.

His scars still write today. They engrave 'Freedom' on the heart of anyone who seeks to be truly identified with Him …

… and that my friends, is a tattoo worth displaying.

Spend a few minutes meditating on today's
key scripture and the devotional, looking
into your own heart … journal what comes
to mind.

Tuesday

The difficulty with blind spots in our lives is … we are blind to them! They are areas other people can see as weak points, but we have become so used to them being in our lives, we have trouble seeing them as anything but 'normal'. Yet when driving, if you make an effort to look at the blind spot, which is the area hidden from our car mirrors, then you will see what otherwise would have been missed.

Lord, thank You for loving me as I am right now. Thank You that I do not need to do anything else to earn Your love – it is there. And yet thank You that Your love for me does not want me to stay in this place. Please help me be self-aware and honest, not digging too deeply but not ignoring the obvious. Show me truth in my life Lord, and as You do, I will become more and more like You – my ultimate desire. Amen.

Read Monday's devotional again, asking the Lord (asking Him out loud often helps one to concentrate) to highlight which areas He wants you to focus on.

Write what comes to mind, or what you are sensing or feeling.

The courage to face D
The fear and shame it holds in
my life. Papa I feel stuck & have
hidden & been afraid for a long
time.

If one word were tattooed on you to describe your life to the watching world, what word would you want that to be and why? (I am not encouraging or discouraging tattoos – it is a hypothetical question for reflection and nothing else.)

Courage - because it is one of the
gifts Papa has placed within you me.
Courage to start again
Today I need courage to face - D

Wednesday

I n driving, a blind spot is defined as: '… areas around the vehicle that cannot be directly observed under existing circumstances.'

And so it is in life; we all have existing circumstances and cultural nuances we have grown up with, or habits which have defined us, which block us from seeing something that is blatantly obvious to others! Finding these blind spots means we need to make a deliberate choice to observe, to ask others if we are missing something, to have a different perspective on a situation, and to adjust where necessary.

How does the Lord usually reveal blind spots – be it habits or sin – to you? (Using others, through the Word, prayer, combination, etc)

If you are unsure, ask Him now to open your eyes to His way of working with you. Ask Him (write out a prayer if you like) to show you the pattern He most often uses in your life.

Papa, how do you reveal blind spots in my life? How do you convict me of sin or things that need to change – please show me – In Jesus Name, Amen.

Let's revisit Monday's key scripture: 'You show that you are a letter from Christ … written not with ink but with the Spirit of the living God, not on tablets of stone but on tablets of human hearts' (2 Cor. 3:3).

If necessary, go back and read the verses surrounding this one – what do you think Paul was saying in this verse?

How we live should be evident that God is in our lives by how we speak, act, react – How we treat other people how we interact with the world around us

If Paul was saying the Corinthian people and their lives revealed the fruit of his ministry, who benefits from the fruit of your ministry? Or who would you like to benefit from it?

my friends, my family, even people I don't know as you talk to them in the passup so many areas.

Thursday

As much as we may desire change in our lives, our blind spots can hinder how easily we accomplish this ourselves.

And this is where the beautiful help of the Holy Spirit comes in. He is wonderful at assisting us as we navigate through the lanes of life, alerting us to potential dangers, and manoeuvring us toward open roads with room to freely roam. He is our partner and our friend, waiting in the wings for His invitation to join us centre stage in this journey.

In John 14:16–17 Jesus says, 'And I will ask the Father, and he will give you another Counsellor to be with you for ever – the Spirit of truth'. The word 'another' in this verse is a Greek word which means literally 'of the same kind and quality'. In other words, Jesus is saying that the Father will send another of the exact kind and quality as Himself to be with us. And that is the precious Holy Spirit who lives inside you (Rom. 8:11)! It is mind boggling to think we have the power of God dwelling within us, ready to lead, guide, counsel, and direct as much as we will give Him control to do so – what a gift!!

Spend some time just praising God for this
wonderful gift of the Holy Spirit. Write out
reasons why you are thankful for the Holy
Spirit's help. (And if you are unfamiliar with the
Holy Spirit, write a prayer instead expressing
your desire to know Him at a deeper level.)

*Gives life power, ever present, full
of grace, peace - brings the fruit
of the Spirit - Wisdom, revelation.*

Read the rest of 2 Corinthians 3 which talks about the
joy of the new covenant (of life since Jesus took our
punishment on the cross and paid the price to free us
from sin and death). Verse 17 is a wonderful verse to
commit to memory. The Amplified Bible puts it like this:
'Now the Lord is the Spirit, and where the Spirit of the
Lord is, there is liberty (emancipation from bondage,
freedom).' Write that verse down a few times, saying it
out loud, committing it to your memory.

Finally, write out what freedom looks like to you
– what does that mean for you as a child of God?

Friday

Finding blind spots is not about becoming paranoid, about hunting for problems, about taking on the role of the Holy Spirit to our spouse and pointing out all *his* blind spots(!), or about deep introspection which never sees the light of day. It is about being sensitive to the leading of the Spirit, always keeping our eyes fixed on Jesus.

In 2 Corinthians 3:18 it says, 'And we, who with unveiled faces all reflect the Lord's glory, are being *transformed into His likeness* with *ever-increasing glory*, which comes from the Lord, who is the Spirit' (emphases mine).

This is a journey, a process which begins from the moment we first asked Jesus to be our Saviour. We *have been* transformed by the blood of Jesus, and we *are being* transformed by His grace – in ever *increasing* glory. Notice it is not decreasing, but increasing!

In 2 Corinthians 5:17 it says, 'Therefore if any person is *[ingrafted] in Christ* (the Messiah) he is a new creation *(a new creature altogether)*; the old [previous moral and spiritual condition] has passed away. Behold, the fresh *and* new has come' (Amplified Bible, emphasis mine)!

What strikes you about the two verses above? How do you feel, thinking about your own life as you read them?

I am grateful that the Holy Spirit convicts. Also very grateful that I am a new creation.

If you are courageous enough, and feel it is right, ask a close friend or spouse if there is a blind spot they see in your life. Then write down what the opposite of that would look like – for example, if the blind spot is pride then the opposite might be humility; if it is stubbornness, then the opposite might be gentleness and servant hood; if it is insecurity, then the opposite might be trust and faith.

Ask Vall —

Hutch
6/9/15.

Is there a Bible verse which could help you in this area? For example, one on humility, servant hood, trust or faith. Write it down and then read it aloud a few times over yourself, declaring it as truth in your life. If you don't know a verse, you could use a concordance to help you, ask a church leader or pray and ask God to show you the right verse for your situation.

Monday

It's Free!

FREEDOM FROM SIN

'So if the Son sets you free, you will be free indeed.' (John 8:36)

'Venti soya latte, extra shot, with Irish cream syrup please.'

It is amazing how the word 'free' modifies one's behaviour.

My normal coffee addiction contains soya milk, but is otherwise a regular size with no extras. (The cost of coffee in London could buy you a small flat in the country, so one has to monitor how many additions are slipped into a coffee order!)

On this occasion though, I asked for all the extras: the biggest size, the extra shot, and even the additional syrup. What was the reason for my sudden extravagance? My punch card was full and this drink was FREE!

If something is free we usually take more than we need, and sometimes even more than we want.

In society today, particularly in the West, we have become so accustomed to paying, we immediately become suspicious of anything 'free'. The old adage

'you can't get something for nothing' comes to mind.

But I fear what society has embraced, Christianity has imbibed. Our culture has created a mindset which says you have to work for reward and that keeping up your guard is necessary, if you want to avoid hurt.

So, how has this affected the Christian Church?

We are often suspicious of freedom. Jesus died, paying the full price, to release total freedom, carrying all the benefits of being the King's kids. Yet how many of us still believe we are unworthy of His love, feel we need to work for His acceptance, or cast judgment on those who are truly enjoying the Christian life?

If I choose to receive all the free benefits of a coffee, how much more should I receive all the free benefits of the cross?

From *that* has come healing, wholeness, forgiveness, redemption, joy, provision, love … Well, the list of options simply does not end with this offer.

Remember – this is a promise which has already been paid.

No punch card required.

Spend time meditating on these truths and ask the Lord if you are walking in the complete freedom He died to give you. Do you find it difficult receiving the free gift of His grace?

Tuesday

Freedom is a gift. One need only ask the person in prison, enslaved, or in fear to know this is true. And it is a gift we have been given in Christ, available to every single one of us if we believe in Him, through His shed blood on the cross, empowering us to actually live free of sin and death – what a thought! Galatians 2:20 says, 'I have been crucified with Christ and I no longer live, but Christ lives in me'. Our old life was crucified to the cross with Christ – that includes all our sin, failures, fears, pain, sickness, abuse, and even death. We are no longer prisoners to any of these things – we are free!

What does Galatians 2:20 mean to you?
– Rewrite it in your own words.

Jacqueline is dead – Jesus lives in me that I may have freedom to live the life I was intended to live with no fear, no condemnation and no rejection.

Do you feel you are fully embracing the gift of
freedom which Christ died to give you? Why or
why not?

No, I fear all that God will take
away - that I consider good in
my life -

Being 'crucified with Christ' does not fluctuate
according to our mood. We ARE crucified with Christ,
even if we don't feel it. Yet often we live our lives
positionally free, whilst personally feeling guilty and
condemned. Can you relate to this? (More on this later
in the week.)

Spend a few minutes confessing any known
sin (don't go digging for it!), repenting, and
receiving God's grace. Imagine that sin left on
the cross, and walk away from it hand in hand
with the risen Christ, knowing you are now
empowered to live as He did when He walked
the earth.

Wednesday

A form of Japanese martial arts is called Aikido. It works by using the momentum of attackers to overcome them and throw them down. In essence, this is what happened at the cross. Christ allowed the enemy to come at Him with all the hatred, sin, and death that he could muster up; and when the enemy threw everything he had at Jesus, Jesus simply used its momentum to overcome death and win a victory. He then took the keys of the kingdom and handed them to us, empowering us to walk with authority and as freely as He did when He walked the earth. It is a mind-boggling thought!

With the Holy Spirit indwelling us, we have the same power which raised Christ from the dead (Rom. 8:11) empowering us to live in victory and freedom here and now.

The victory of the cross is found in the power of the resurrection. Spend some time praising and thanking Christ for what He did at the Cross – write out your prayer of thanks.

....

....

....

....

Jesus walked with authority, but He also walked in love. Our freedom is not only for our benefit, but in order that we might see His kingdom come here on earth – and we are part of that! Who could use your love and encouragement? In what way will you show that today? (text, note, letter, email)

What are some ways you could bring His kingdom to your area of influence? In other words, are there other ways you could walk as Jesus did – in your neighbourhood, at your job, within your family?

....

....

....

....

....

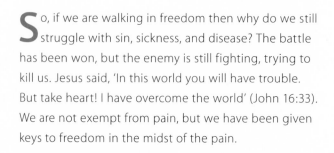

Thursday

S o, if we are walking in freedom then why do we still struggle with sin, sickness, and disease? The battle has been won, but the enemy is still fighting, trying to kill us. Jesus said, 'In this world you will have trouble. But take heart! I have overcome the world' (John 16:33). We are not exempt from pain, but we have been given keys to freedom in the midst of the pain.

Recently I read a phrase I really liked: 'we must die to what has killed us.' In other words, whatever the enemy has used to bring hurt, death or destruction into our lives is exactly what needs to be left on the cross of Jesus Christ. We must die to it there, and walk away in the freedom granted through Christ.

What do you think of this? How does this phrase apply to your life?

. . . .

. . . .

. . . .

. . . .

. . . .

Often we will believe we have been crucified with Him, believe that we are free, yet still choose to live bound in the sin and bad habits which keep us from a fulfilled life of freedom. Paul alluded to this in Romans 7:15–25.

Read and rewrite these verses (summarise them) in your own words. *And notice that Paul ends by recognising that Jesus Christ, on the cross, is what has saved him from this tyranny of sin!*

....

....

....

....

....

Declare over yourself 'I am free because of the cross!' – say it as many times as necessary to begin to feel your spirit rejoicing in this truth. You ARE free in Christ and through the cross! Write out a prayer of thanksgiving to the Lord.

Friday

Though God has given us freedom, we still must choose to live it out in our daily lives. We can do this by fully embracing it, living from the mindset of a free woman in Christ, or we can limit our experience of freedom by seeing sin and death as more powerful and controlling than the freedom we have been given. Often it is not a deliberate choice to limit freedom in this way, and the best way to change is by actively seeking to break habits of wrong thinking.

Christ died to set us free and we can choose to *fully* embrace that lifestyle of freedom by what we believe, say, and eventually do.

Take time to read Romans 8 today. Write down key verses which jump out at you. Let the words sink deep into your spirit. Then after reading and thinking about this passage in regards to your life right now, journal your other thoughts.

Monday

Hidden Treasures

FREEDOM FROM UNFORGIVENESS

'"Lord, how many times shall I forgive my brother when he sins against me? Up to seven times?" Jesus answered, "I tell you, not seven times, but seventy-seven times."' (Matt. 18:21–22)

'Spend £10 and get one bag of cow foot free'

Yep, that was the actual banner across the front of the corner shop, and it was not a joke. I did a double take, not really certain I had read it correctly. Cow feet? I mean, lovely that they are free, but … cow's feet!

To someone else this sign may have proved enticing; to me it was simply confusing. Because although I have seen cow's feet, and all things being relative they are not that unattractive, I have never actually tasted one. I am certain in the right environment and with the correct flavouring they are delicious, but in my realm of experience I simply have no compartment in which to store this information.

What tempts one person, may drive away another.

Which then begs the question: What entices me? And what repulses me? And would it match Jesus' list (imagining He had kept one in His back pocket)?

Jesus wasn't impressed by rules as much as relationship; He wasn't captivated by status as much as the servant heart; He was repulsed by the proud, religious person whilst He embraced the humble, embarrassed prostitute. Those in pain caught His eye, those in position felt His words.

Do I stand against injustice, offering healing to the helpless and ministering grace to the hopeless? Or am I captivated by the comfortable, playing it safe within my own culture, opposing anyone who may appear different from myself?

I want to live like Jesus who was drawn in by compassion and poured out by love.

But to do this I must first resist judgment of what I do not comprehend, *for the heart of God is often found in the areas we fear to understand.*

Those very areas, or people, wait for us to draw near; challenging us to look beyond their palpable banners of hurt and hopelessness into the treasure which lives inside.

Spend a few minutes asking God to speak
to your heart this week about prejudices
you may be carrying – against a person,
group of people, or place. Unforgiveness
and bitterness are seeds of destruction
in our own hearts. May this be the time
the Lord can reveal, and then gently heal,
what has been carried around with you
long enough. Be bold and courageous in
allowing Him to do this!

Tuesday

Everyone asks the same questions: Do you love me?
Do you need me?

I heard a pastor say that once and it resonated with me.
All of us cry out for recognition, love, and acceptance
from the moment we are born until the moment we
take our last breath. We long to be loved and to have
purpose in our being here on earth; to know that our
lives mattered for something.

Do you agree with the above statement that everyone
asks these two very important questions? In what way
do you see yourself asking these questions?

**If you were to write out a purpose statement
for your life, what would it say (or at least what
key words would it include)?**

Love you Papa with my whole heart
and love those around me you
bring into my life.

What words do people close to you use to describe you? If we are struggling to identify our gifts or know our purpose, sometimes listening to these words can actually help bring clarity. If you are bold, ask a close friend or relative the top five words they would use to describe you!

loving, strong, compassionate, open, honest. Funny, caring, joyful, bright, intelligent, happy.

Father, thank You for making me with purpose and having a plan for my life! I know that sometimes it feels like I am going in circles, yet I trust that You can use me where I am at right now to bring You glory. I pray Father that You would uncover any hidden gifts in my life, and that You would give me opportunities to use the gifts I have already discovered, to bless others. As I mature in my understanding of who You are, expand my territory Lord and let me experience, at an even deeper level, the joy of serving and loving You! Amen!

Wednesday

Early in life we may believe lies about ourselves because of bad experiences or how we have been treated and those lies can result in wounds which fester for years. A parent speaks harshly to us and we believe we are not significant, a relative abuses the trust we had in them and we feel ashamed, a classmate labels us incorrectly yet we take their words over what we know to be true. Suddenly the lies we have received early in life become the wounds from which we respond later in life.

Take some time to pray and ask the Holy Spirit to reveal any lies you have believed about yourself or about others in the past. Give Him time to answer and write down what you hear.

The lie I have believed is
that I am not wanted
and I have believed this my
whole life.

If we have believed a lie about ourselves, we
often will have a wound attached to that lie.
Again, take some time asking the Holy Spirit to
reveal any wounds you have experienced as a
result of a lie believed, and record anything you
hear or sense.

See journal
Sept 16ʰ 2015

Then simply ask the Father what is the truth?
Ask Him to tell you how much He loves you.
Write down any words, pictures, or senses
you have from this. Give Him freedom to love
you – He longs to do that and welcomes any
opportunity we give Him to reach into our daily
lives and bless, 'hug', and encourage us!

Thursday

Each person has a story to tell, and each story has painful pages, along with the good, which help make up the whole. The one on the street, the one in the supermarket, the one who betrayed you, the one spreading gossip, the one appearing lazy, the one taking advantage – each fragile life includes at least a few dashed hopes and unseen dreams. It does not excuse wrong behaviour, but it does remind us that we are all human and on a journey together.

The writer Debbie Ford once said unforgiveness is like 'the poison you drink every day hoping that the other person will die'. So true. It will only destroy us, never the one who caused us the pain.

Have you ever experienced a time in your life when you struggled to forgive? Or is there currently anyone you are struggling to forgive? What has made it so difficult?

In light of that, what do you think about the statement, 'Unforgiveness is like drinking poison and expecting the other person to die'?

Forgiveness is not about setting the perpetrator free, it is about setting ourselves free. And sometimes we need to forgive several times – in one day! – in order to remain in that freedom. Forgiveness is a choice, not a feeling. Ask the Holy Spirit to reveal to you if there is anyone you still need to forgive for an offence done to you, and record their name(s) …

If you are able and willing, pray the following prayer of forgiveness:

Father, thank You for forgiving me for all I have done wrong and the times I have hurt or judged others. Your compassion is never-ending and Your mercies are new every morning, and for that I am so grateful. I struggle sometimes to give the same compassion and mercy to others, but today I am choosing to change that. I ask for Your forgiveness where I have held onto bitterness, resentment, and sometimes hatred, toward [insert names] and I now choose to forgive _____ for [insert what he/she/they did]. I release them and ask that You would bless them, not for what they have done but because You are a God of love. I put the cross of Jesus Christ between _____ and myself. I pray this in the name of Jesus Christ, Amen.

Friday

Walking in forgiveness is walking in freedom; it is to see people through a different lens and to release them to be who God created them to be, allowing them to choose free from our accusations and judgments. In the meantime, it allows you to carry on in the destiny created specifically for you. God will make a way. No man can destroy His plans and purposes; He will always watch over those whose hearts are toward Him, and His ways are always good.

Let us learn to follow Jesus' example: a man who walked in complete forgiveness, therefore who walked in total freedom.

'Whoever claims to live in him must walk as Jesus did.' (I John 2:6)

You may need to read the prayer on the preceding page and walk through the steps of forgiveness again. Do it as many times as necessary; when done from the heart, there will eventually be a day where it gets easier and the pain appears less.

Imagine a clear glass of water, and bitterness as bits of dirt. Ask the Holy Spirit to show you what your heart looks like – is it clear, or are there any areas of bitterness to be cleaned out? If He reveals areas, repent and bless those you were feeling bitter toward.

God is love. Today, intentionally choose to love the unlovable. Maybe this means praying for someone you struggle with, visiting someone you find difficult, reaching out to someone on the street, or showing compassion to the person in the office who shows no compassion for anyone else. Ask God who it is – then go be a blessing!

Monday

Stalemate

FREEDOM FROM STAGNATION

'This resurrection life you received from God is not a timid, grave-tending life. It's adventurously expectant, greeting God with a childlike "What's next Papa?"' (Romans 8:15, The Message)

Stalemate.

Admittedly I know nothing about chess; yet I have
heard that stalemate is not the desired position at the
end of a game.

I also know there are times in life when we feel at a
stalemate, or possibly even choose stalemate, thinking
it better to draw than to fail.

Most of us know people who have become, in some
area, comfortable in their stalemate. They remain stuck
– either ignorant of a different outcome or frozen in
place, fearing what change might mean. Fear has the
ability to keep us locked in a position we should have
left long ago.

The religious crowd in the Bible (the Pharisees and
Sadducees) held tightly to the law, believing that by
doing so they would win favour with God. They held
onto it so tightly, however, that life itself was extracted
from their relationship with God and spiritual death by
rules became the norm. To join them meant living a life
of bondage, yet to leave them, in their eyes, meant you
were choosing a life of sin.

Jesus moved the stalemate.

In dying on the cross and making the law obsolete,
He brought a fresh choice and new life (John 10:10),
opening up a place we scarcely believed existed – true
FREEDOM. We now have freedom to fail without fear of
losing His love – He *is* love (1 John 4:16) and that Love
will never leave us or forsake us (Heb. 13:5; Deut. 31:6).
We also now have freedom to risk without fear of what
failure may mean – our identity being in Him, not in
our success (Col. 3:3; Rom. 8:37; 1 John 4:4).

(Grace to let go !)

When I know acceptance by my heavenly Father is
already assured, I am free to risk, knowing *success is in
the risk taken, not the outcome achieved.* And from the
position of risking without fear of failure, comes the
privilege of failing without fear of condemnation.

I encourage you to move away from any position
of stalemate and invite the Holy Spirit to come and
occupy your situation, life, dreams, and pain; bringing
new life and new hope for the better place in your
future. He always desires good things for us and He
always gives good gifts because He is a GOOD God …
a King who will never be put in a corner.

Take a few minutes to ponder this
devotional – what does it say to you today?
Are there any areas of fear the Lord may
want you to look at this week? How would
you define freedom?

Tuesday

S tagnant waters collect debris and lose the essence of their vitality. It would surprise nobody that the Dead Sea is, in reality, dead; life cannot be sustained in a place which by its very nature suffocates. Yet many of us try to live a spiritual life filled with vitality, whilst swimming in a sea of religion.

The Pharisees and Sadducees were bound up by rules and religion. Following the law became more important than loving the Lord. It was what they knew, it was familiar, and it had firm boundaries which were immovable. Suddenly Jesus came on the scene and everything was turned upside down. No longer were the rules clear, the boundaries fixed, or the mandates memorised – now love was more important than legalities and tradition was trumped by grace. Confusion reigned in the camp as the playing field once again became level – men, women, Jew, Gentile, slave, free – all were loved the same (Gal. 3:28). And this radical change was at times a bit too much for the religious rule-keepers.

How would you describe the difference between religion and a relationship (with God)?

Are there areas in your spiritual life where it feels stagnant and lifeless? If so, ask the Lord to show you if there are any religious activities which may look good on the outside, but inwardly they are removing vitality and spiritual life. Write down anything you sense, hear, or feel.

I'm struggling in prayer - Want to pray in the spirit not from my head, but my heartfully engaged with the Holy Spirit.

How do you think the religious crowd (Pharisees and Sadducees) felt when Jesus helped the Gentiles (non-Jews), such as the Samaritan woman (John 4:1–26) or the Syro-Phoenician woman (Mark 7:24–30)? Is there anyone you would not want Jesus to help, heal or set free? *~~Would Osama Bin Laden~~ . No*

If you answered 'yes' to the previous question, is this an area of unforgiveness? Might you need (again) to forgive someone for hurting you? *No* Forgiveness is an act of the will; it is a choice and not a feeling. Ask God to help you forgive and then bless (as a choice) the person you least would like to see Him bless.

Wednesday

The game which the religious ironically thought they had won suddenly showed them in positions of stalemate. It could be likened to reaching the top of a ladder, only to find it was leaning against the wrong wall! They thought they were advancing and gaining 'spiritual promotion points' by adhering to all the rules, only to discover their abundance of rules and judgment simply cemented them into a place of deeper bondage.

Jesus Christ died to set us free, not to limit us, but to release us into the fullness of LIFE and life abundant! When we allow circumstances, fears, sin, shame, or the judgment of others to dictate our destiny, we have stepped into a stagnant sea of debris which will eventually cloud the clarity we once had.

If inner freedom was a 10 on the following scale, where would you put yourself? Why?

1 _____ 10

Ask the Holy Spirit to reveal to you any area of judgment you are harbouring, which you may not see. Write down what you hear, sense, or feel.

. . . .

. . . .

. . . .

. . . .

If there is judgment in your heart, repent and ask the Lord to forgive you. If it is toward a certain person or persons, ask the Lord to bless them – pray for them as you would want someone to pray for you.

Spend a few minutes meditating on the life of Jesus and how He spent it, with whom He spent His time, and those He healed and to whom He gave attention. Remember the disciples were ordinary men with ordinary jobs and that Jesus let women near and around Him in a culture which gave no value to women. He was touched by lepers and He touched the dead, to see them raised up again – all acts which broke the religious laws of the day. Ask the Lord to break your heart for the hurting, open your eyes to the distressed, and show you the ones He wants *you* to touch.

Thursday

ill you trust that the love of God can be greater
W *than the fear of man or strength of sin?*

Repentance is a beautiful gift and if we have lived trying to please anyone else but God, we have stepped into pride. In fact, if we are striving to please even God we have stepped into pride. Anything done apart from the grace and empowerment of the Father is dangerously close to arrogance, control, insecurity, or fear – all of which, ultimately, have their roots in pride.

Write out your own definition of pride here. Then ask the Lord to show you where pride may be lurking in the corners of your own heart.

Pride - any place in my heart or life where I try to add to what God has done for me in Christ Jesus or any place I try to please others rather than Papa!

Repentance is nothing to be ashamed of; it is a gift to be embraced! God does not want us 'navel gazing' and constantly looking for areas of sin and error in our own lives. But as the Holy

Spirit brings up areas to address, we can do it in humility and thankfulness for the cross and the grace of God. Write out a prayer of thankfulness here to the Lord – thanking Him for His grace, favour, blessings – anything you want really!

....

....

....

....

....

Read aloud the Lord's Prayer (Matt. 6:9–15) and write down which verse(s) jumps out at you. Spend time meditating on the truths listed there: holiness of God, kingdom living, provision, forgiveness, strength to overcome temptation, etc.

....

....

....

....

....

Friday

We are in Christ and Christ is in the Father, (John 14:6–14) and secure in their love is our place of identity and rest. Fear cannot cohabitate with rest; neither can striving, strife, control, insecurity, passivity, or pride. All of those will eventually bring death; only in rest will we find life and victory.

From that place, whichever move we make, God can work it out for our good (Rom. 8:28). For what He has started, He has promised to finish (Phil. 1:6), if we trust Him with all our heart, leaning not on our understanding, but in all of our ways acknowledging Him (Prov. 3:5–6).

What do you think it means to be 'in Christ'? What does it mean to you?

It means that nothing can seperate me from Papa's love. It means that I am secure — happy, free!

What are the areas which keep you from remaining in a place of rest and peace? Or do you feel you have learned the secret of rest – and if so, what is it?

Insecurity – that I am not wanted !

Trust can be a difficult, yet beautiful, exercise of our faith. What does the phrase 'in all your ways acknowledge him' (Prov. 3:5) mean to you and how can you do that?
(I encourage you to share this with someone who can hold you accountable to trusting Him in this new area.)

Reread Monday's devotional, thinking of the areas you want to forgive, trust and release.

Spend a few minutes envisioning new life being poured into your spirit – imagine it as fresh water poured from heaven into you. Receive His grace, forgiveness, and refreshment and choose to move from stagnation of fear to saturation in faith!

Monday

Thanks, Dad

FREEDOM FROM SELF-PITY

'Consider it pure joy, my brother,
whenever you face trials of many
kinds, because you know that
the testing of your faith develops
perseverance. (James 1:2)

'But daddy, I CAN'T!'

'Just – try, try again!'

If I heard those words once, I heard them a thousand times growing up. My father was a master encourager, always advising the 'once more' as opposed to the 'once tried'. And here was I, his red-headed little girl who preferred being served by others to working hard … and of course, sporting the ultimate pout when I didn't get my way. Parenting me was an uphill battle at times!

Words have power and we will reap what has been sown. My father not only spoke the words to me, he lived them in his own life. A prime example of this came recently when, at seventy years of age, my father led a team of one other adult and four teenagers hiking in the Porcupine Mountains of Northern Michigan – a journey of more than thirty miles carrying a backpack weighing forty-five pounds (nearly twenty-three kilos) on his back.

Lesson? Amongst other obvious ones … don't give up.

I don't know what you are struggling with today or
what is threatening your spiritual journey, but the end
has not yet come. I firmly believe if you are breathing,
your purpose has not yet been fulfilled.

When Jesus carried His cross toward Golgotha, He
buckled under the weight, so Simon, from Cyrene,
took up the burden for Him (Matt. 27:32) and Jesus
fulfilled His mission. When the Jews were about to
be annihilated and fear was rampant, Queen Esther
prayed, fasted and trusted in the plan of God
(Esth. 4:15–16) and a nation was saved. When Peter
denied the Lord and humiliated himself, Jesus sought
Him out for reconciliation (John 21:15–19) and 3,000
people became believers a few weeks later.

Things may look difficult at the moment and the road
may be filled with potholes and stumbling stones,
but the hand of God is never out of reach. As a good
Father, He is there to help you when you falter and
cheer you on when you succeed. I learned this first
from my earthly father and later it was confirmed by
my heavenly Father.

You know … I think my dad *and* my Dad are both pretty wise.

And this is one red-head (OK, slightly less red with age) who is trying to do less pouting and more listening!

Take a few minutes and ponder the following question: Is there anything God is asking you to do which you have been putting off doing? If so, what is the first step toward seeing it done?

Tuesday

When was the last time you mumbled those ever so addictive words – 'I can't' – to yourself? And what was the result? For most of us, it was a self-fulfilling declaration which brought about little or no positive outcome. In other words – we didn't!

Self-pity was one of my closest friends and allies for many years. We were on first-name basis with each other, had each other on speed dial, visited often, had many pity parties together where we invited lots of other friends like depression, fear, despair and regret, and never let too much time pass before one of us tried to get in touch. In many ways, we were inseparable! Yet self-pity was anything but a true friend; it was a wolf in sheep's clothing and one who did not play fair.

In which areas/situations do you find yourself most tempted toward self-pity?

When I feel rejected – then I live in a much loanlier derker world.

What are some other choices you can make in those moments, as opposed to repeating the same cycle of self-pity again? (phoning a friend, praying, exercise)

Choosing to do what it says in Phil 4:8.

Write down a few sentences of 'wise words' you received growing up from a man who was influential in your life; possibly a father, grandfather, pastor or friend. What comes to mind?

Know something about everything and everything about something (John Steerer).

Wednesday

Living in a state of self-pity will only breed isolation, depression, insecurity, self-centeredness, jealousy and a host of other barriers to one's personal destiny and purpose. At times it appears justified, especially when life throws us pain due to no fault of our own, yet I assure you it is never life-giving. Self-pity will always take more than it appears to give and will always leave its victim in a place of despair, never hope.

So why do we enjoy having it around? Because it soothes our flesh and tells us that we have 'rights'. We have a right to feel angry because someone has wrongly accused us; or to harbour bitterness because we have been betrayed; or to be depressed because an illness is destroying our health; or to hate because of the depth of abuse we endured. The list of reasons to pity ourselves is endless; and I guarantee the enemy will ensure it stays regularly updated. He knows how effectively it can keep us from living the abundant life that Jesus came to give us.

Are there any areas in your life you have felt/feel you have a 'right' to self-pity? Is there anyone you still need to forgive because they have caused you pain which has led to the cycle of pity?

Forgiveness is a powerful gift and tool we have been given to set ourselves free. And forgiveness is a choice made, in often difficult circumstances, to free ourselves from carrying offence whilst also pleading the case for another to receive mercy. Possibly doing this devotional has brought to mind a situation which has kept you in self-pity and now you need to choose instead to forgive. You may already have used the prayer of forgiveness earlier in this devotional but it is very important to be honest. If this is an area you are struggling with, pray once more:

Father God, thank You for graciously giving me forgiveness by shedding Your own blood on the cross. I choose now to forgive [insert name] for [insert what he/she did] and ask that the situation be covered by the blood of Jesus. I ask for mercy instead of justice and declare that I will not hold this against _____. I choose to bless _____ and ask for healing over this entire situation. Thank You for giving me the ability to forgive and I choose to release myself from the need for any retribution, in the name of Jesus. Amen.

Then spend a few minutes worshiping the Lord and thanking Him for the forgiveness He has shown to you! If it helps, write out a prayer of thanksgiving to Him.

Thursday

Holding onto unforgiveness, bitterness, or any other form of self-pity will never bring us true freedom. It may feel good to our flesh and we may enjoy crying over a cup of tea whilst bemoaning our lot in life, but it will never get us out of our rut and onto the road of freedom. Are there times for tears? *Definitely.* Yet we must never allow tears to morph into pity, which inevitably transforms itself into a prison.

Living free means living released from our rights. Jesus said that He only did what His Father asked Him to do and only said what His Father asked Him to say (John 12:49–50; 14:31). He never asked for special treatment because of who He was. The apostle Paul, who wrote the majority of the New Testament, called himself 'the worst' of all sinners (1 Tim. 1:15) – not because he had a poor self-image, but because he realised the depth of grace, and joy of freedom. He had many reasons to beat himself up, knowing he had killed many innocent people when he was blind to the truth, yet instead Paul chose the path of humility, which consequently landed him on the path of freedom.

Read the verses referred to above in your own Bible and spend a few minutes meditating on the relationship between Jesus and His Father.

How is your relationship with the Father similar/
different? How would you like it to change?

*I would like to do only what the father
told me to do too.*

Read Philippians 2:1–11 to see how Jesus
modelled humility. What do you feel God wants
to say to you through this today? In what ways
do you feel you do this well? In what ways might
you need to improve? Pause and ask the Holy
Spirit to speak clearly to you.

*Want to learn to walk by the Holy
Spirit.*

Write out a list of at least ten things for which
you are thankful. Try to make them specific – for
example, not things like food, shelter or family. As
wonderful as those things are, the more specific
we can be with our thanks, the more heartfelt it
often is. Take as much time as you'd like!

① I am thankful –   to be alive,
② I am thankful God can change me.
③ I am thankful God loves me
④ I am thankful God has a plan and
⑤ purpose for me.
⑥ I am thankful I am not alone.
⑦ I am thankful for Gods grace
⑧ and mercy.   ⑨ I am thankful for
*   freedom.*

10) I am thankful for choice.

Friday

Self-pity was a good friend, but once unmasked I recognised it for what it actually was – an enemy. *Repentance was my pathway toward freedom*. And I actually discovered that repentance makes a much better party guest than self-pity ever does!

If you find yourself caught up in the self-pity cycle, remember the words of my father who would simply say: 'Try, try again'. And of course, remember as well the words of my heavenly Father who reminds us, 'I can do everything through him who gives me strength' (Phil. 4:13) and 'So if the Son sets you free, you will be free indeed' (John 8:36).

Wise words indeed.

Take a moment to read Monday's devotional once again, and write down anything new that jumps out to you from it this time.

'Consider it pure joy, my brother, whenever you face trials of many kinds, because you know the testing of your faith develops perseverance (James 1:2)

After taking time this week to look at this whole area, is there a place where you feel you need to 'try, try again'? Maybe with a friend/ spouse/family member? Or with your job? Or by beginning to dream and hope again in an area where hope has faded away?

To dream again .

Allow me to pray this for you today:

Father, I pray for the one reading this devotional – that she would know how very much she is loved and adored by You. I ask now that Your presence would surround her and I pray for revelation of Your grace and Your acceptance of her. I pray for a restoration of hope and freedom in any area of bondage which has resulted from self-pity. Father, please open new doors, breathe in new life, and show her new beginnings. We trust You, Lord for You are GOOD and You are LOVE. Amen.

Finish by reading Proverbs 3:5–6 and declaring that over your own life and situation!

Monday

To Kiss or Not to Kiss ...

FREEDOM FROM THE WORLD

'Our Father in heaven, hallowed be your name, your kingdom come, your will be done on earth as it is in heaven.' (Matt. 6:9–10)

... that is the question.

Moving to another culture opened the floodgates to new information, 'strange' habits, and more than my share of embarrassing mishaps. Receiving my indefinite leave to remain not only solidified my desire to stay in England, it was also testimony of surviving cultural integration with a society vastly (yes, it really is!) different from the US where I grew up. So, one would think after this many years I would have grasped the basic cultural nuances.

Wrong.

An anomaly which still invokes fear and trepidation at any given moment is the greeting. There are times you greet one another with a kiss on the cheek, followed by a hug; other times it is only a hug; and sometimes a handshake is sufficient. Yet on some occasions a kiss on both cheeks with no hug takes place; and the rarest of instances (which I embarrassingly messed up once) provides a three-time kiss on alternating cheeks. With the plethora of options, how is one to choose? And because this applies to both men and women, it seriously complicates the issue. If you are friends

with a guy do you still kiss him on the cheek, or is that
sending the wrong message? What if someone is going
for a kiss on the cheek and you are reaching for a hug –
the amount of hair I have eaten over the past ten years
would produce a lion size hairball!

Getting used to a new culture takes time. It takes
patience. It takes a sense of humour. And it takes a
willingness to adapt.

No wonder we struggle at times to see and believe
the 'kingdom of God' culture here on earth (Matt. 6:10;
16:19; Luke 12:32–34). But if we call ourselves Christians,
shouldn't this culture become more real than the
natural one in which we find ourselves?

On some days it feels tangible, but on many days it
feels uncomfortable.

Forgive. Love (*everyone*). Serve. Trust. Pray. Give.
Honour. Believe. Forgive … everyone.

This describes the kingdom in which I was created to
dwell (Gen. 1:27) and on my good days these are the
lenses through which I choose to view life.

The 'culture clash' may be an ongoing challenge, but I am learning that *the more I live from God's kingdom perspective because I choose to, the less I conform to the world's perspective because I have to.*

Now, if only salutations were that simple …

Spend some time pondering the kingdom of heaven; Jesus instructed us to pray His kingdom come, His will be done on earth as it is in heaven – what does that mean to you?

Tuesday

Have you ever felt out of place, like a round peg in a square hole? Or felt that you were a fake and at some point in life you were going to be found out for not really being the person everyone thought you were?

I think at one point or another in life we all feel or have felt that way. There is such pressure in society today to conform to an idealised norm. 'They' (whoever they are!) tell us what is fashionable, what is acceptable, what is politically correct, how to speak, how to act and even how to raise our children! And going against culturally acceptable regulations immediately puts us on the outside looking in.

Jesus said in John 17:15–16, 'My prayer is not that you take them out of the world but that you protect them from the evil one. They are not of the world, even as I am not of it'. We are in the world, but we are not of it. And we have been given everything we need to live a godly, overcoming life here and now.

In what area(s) of your life do you feel the most pressure to conform?

Church -

Do you find it difficult to stand against what others say is acceptable if you don't feel it is right? Why or why not?

Because I think people think they know Gods mind from reading scripture that isn't there.

In the above scripture Jesus says, 'They are not of the world, even as I am not of it.' What do you think He meant by that and how is that practically demonstrated in your daily life?

I think it's changing as God changes me life becomes less about the flesh & people and more about God and relationship with Him.

Wednesday

Jesus was a law-breaker. The Pharisees had taken the Commandments given by God and added 613 different oral laws people needed to obey. On several occasions Jesus chose to disregard the man-made law and instead act out of a higher law – the law of love. Some examples of Jesus breaking the law include: healing on the Sabbath (Luke 13:10–17), letting His disciples eat with unwashed hands (Mark 7:1–23) and speaking to the Samaritan woman (John 4:1–26).

Jesus said to the Pharisees, 'You have let go of the commands of God and are holding on to the traditions of men' (Mark 7:8).

Have you ever intentionally broken the law (eg speeding)? Do you believe breaking the law was/is ever justified in God's eyes?

Ask the Holy Spirit to reveal if there are any
areas in your own life where tradition has
superseded the commands of God. Write down
what you hear.

....
....
....
....
....

Why is it easier to hold onto tradition rather
than walk in love? What does walking in love
require from us?

....
....
....
....
....

Thursday

Replacing grace with law comes easily. Having rules which need to be obeyed is much easier than having freedom which can be interpreted. Yet God chose from the beginning to give us free will – freedom to choose.

Jesus chose love; loving God first and foremost and loving His neighbour after that (read Matt. 22:37–40).

How would this world change if we let love, grace and forgiveness be the leading factors in our daily lives? How would our families change? Our work places? Are we so busy defending ourselves and our rights that we have lost the first and greatest commandment of all?

God has given us free will so that we are not robots – programmed, with no ability to choose for ourselves. It is a gift!

Are you comfortable with free will in your own life, or would part of you prefer 'rules'? Why or why not?

In what way do you practically 'love your neighbour as yourself'? Or, what way would you like to improve on that? (Remember 'neighbour' is not necessarily the person next door, it is whoever God brings across your path at any point in time.)

....

....

....

....

....

Reread Matthew 22:37–40. Write out various ways you can love the Lord with your
1) heart, 2) soul, 3) mind – think of at least three suggestions for each!

....

....

....

....

....

Friday

If we truly want His kingdom to come, it begins with us and how we love. That is a 'law' which never fails, and one which works in every culture of the world.

The end of Monday's devotional said this: *the more I live from God's kingdom perspective because I choose to, the less I conform to the world's perspective because I have to.*

What does that statement mean to you?

One is free choice the other is not.

God's love endures forever

inspire

...ays do you see yourself conforming to ...more than to the kingdom of God?

....

....

....

....

....

Reread the Lord's Prayer in Matthew 6:9–13 taking time to think about each line and what it means to you. Imagine the Father, meditate on His holy name, imagine His kingdom here on earth, thank Him for His provision, asking Him if there is anyone to forgive. Let these beautiful, timeless truths speak new life into your spirit today.

Monda

We give thanks to You, O God.

Ps. 75:1

inspire

Are You Undignified?

FREEDOM FROM CONFORMING

'David said to Michal, "… I will celebrate before the LORD. I will become even more undignified than this, and I will be humiliated in my own eyes."' (2 Sam. 6:21–22)

I love those verses.

David was celebrating the return of the ark of the covenant into the city of David. He was praising. He was rejoicing. He was ecstatic. He was embarrassing.

His wife was humiliated. She was ashamed of his antics, uncomfortable with his joy and angry at his loud, wild, radical, display of pleasure regarding the presence of God. So what was David's response? Basically he said: 'I've been chosen to lead others. I lead by example, and I will show them that the presence of God brings out the radical inside each of us.' Well – that's my interpretation at least!

David was not worried about the people, because he was overwhelmed with the presence. *He knew it was not possible to touch the glory of God, and walk away the same.* He learned this from Moses who was asked to remove his shoes, and later avert his eyes, due to the immense power of glory (Exod. 3:5; 33:19–23).

Have you allowed God's presence to change you?
To transform your behaviour?

The glory in the ark affected the worshipper in David. Hundreds of years later, the glory in the Man influenced sinners around Jesus. A few thousand years on, the glory of the Spirit longs to shape society through you and me.

David chose worship over a whining wife, praise over potential embarrassment and undignified dancing, which brought untold glory to the One he loved. Embarrassing?

No – *empowering.*

Take some time to think about how you express love. Have you ever embarrassed yourself for another? For the Lord? What was the outcome?

Tuesday

People in love do strange things.

They act in ways which ordinarily might get them sectioned, but when love is involved their actions receive approval! For example, look at a father in love with his child. He makes all sorts of crazy faces and strange noises, which in any other environment would have people crossing the road in avoidance. But when in love – it's acceptable and endearing!

Or couples who look longingly into the eyes of the other, completely oblivious to anyone else who might be standing in the room. The intensity of the stares would normally cause another person to flee in fear, but when it comes from being smitten, all is forgiven.

We are not afraid to show love to a child or a lover, yet when it comes to expressing love for God we tend to retreat into shyness. I find politically correct expression nauseating. Why is one form of expression considered acceptable, whilst another is over the top? And who is the judge? God looks at the heart, not the outward appearance. One person can appear to be worshipping with all her heart, yet be thinking of the roast cooking at home; whilst another is outwardly contemplative, yet inwardly lost in love.

Reread Monday's devotional and think about your own expression of worship. Has it changed over the years? Do you wish it would be different somehow? If there was one thing you could change, what would it be?

....

....

....

God is crazy in love with you. THAT is a fact. In what ways do you feel He makes His love tangible to you? If you struggle to answer that question, ask the Holy Spirit to help you identify what you may not be able to see at the moment.

....

....

....

Close your eyes and imagine looking into the eyes of Christ. Linger on that for a while, ask the Lord to show you Himself, then write down what you see/sense/feel.

....

....

....

....

Wednesday

Amidst our relative society, the world thrives on conforming. Even the self-named misfits seek a tribe to call home; we all long to belong to someone.

Jesus was not a conformist; He was a man of love. And that love took on whatever form was needed at that moment. Sometimes it looked normal, like hugging a child. Most times it looked appalling, like touching a prostitute. He was willing to be undignified in order to express the love of His Father to a loveless society.

Are we willing to do the same?

Jesus was a friend of sinners and regularly broke the Pharisaic law by doing things like those we mentioned last week when we looked at Him being a law-breaker. And yet He was without sin. Reread Galatians chapter 3 and write down what you observe as being different between the law and faith.

Consider those observations. How do they relate to you today? Are there things you do which have their source in religion, not in relationship with the Lord?

....

....

....

....

....

What do you think about the fact that Jesus was not a conformist? How can you identify with that?

....

....

....

....

....

Thursday

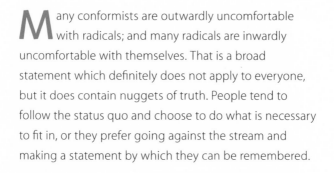

M any conformists are outwardly uncomfortable with radicals; and many radicals are inwardly uncomfortable with themselves. That is a broad statement which definitely does not apply to everyone, but it does contain nuggets of truth. People tend to follow the status quo and choose to do what is necessary to fit in, or they prefer going against the stream and making a statement by which they can be remembered.

Jesus did neither. He was not concerned with the status quo and He did not live to please man (John 2:24); nor did He rebel simply for the sake of rebellion and making a statement. He did not live to please man; He lived for another agenda altogether.

Would you describe yourself more as a conformist or a radical? Or are you a bit of both? Or neither? Has that changed over the years and if so why?

When was the last time you shared your faith with someone? If this is difficult for you to do, what is the greatest fear which keeps you from doing this?

....
....
....
....
....

Write a prayer asking the Lord to help you in this area of living to please God and not man. Confess what is most difficult for you, repent if necessary, and then ask the Lord to empower you to live differently in the future. Make it personal and honest. Ask Him if there is anyone today to whom He would like you to 'be Jesus' in a new way.

....
....
....
....
....

Friday

L et's finish the week meditating on God's presence!
Reread this devotional paragraph:

> David was not worried about the people because he
> was overwhelmed with the presence. *He knew it was*
> *not possible to touch the glory of God, and walk away*
> *the same.* He learned this from Moses who was asked
> to remove his shoes, and later avert his eyes, due to
> the immense power of glory (Exod. 3:5; 33:19–23).

Today, spend five to ten minutes focusing on the
presence of Almighty God. If you are able, close
your eyes and use your imagination to focus on His
characteristics, His love, and maybe even His features
– imagine the eyes of Jesus looking at you, the hands
of Jesus healing you … When your mind begins to
wander, just pull it back again.

Have a piece of paper next to you so that if you
suddenly remember something which needs to be
done, or that you don't want to forget, you can write it
down, then go back to meditating on Jesus.

If you are finding it difficult to focus for so long, begin by saying out loud various characteristics of God that you love: His grace, freedom, love, patience, joy and kindness. Keep your eyes closed, but meditate on those characteristics.

Get lost in love.

It is a beautiful place to explore and He will always welcome you there …

Monday

Dance

FREEDOM FROM ANXIETY

'Don't fret or worry. Instead of worrying
pray. Let petitions and praises shape
your worries into prayers, letting
God know your concerns.'
(Phil.4:6–7, The Messsage)

'Put on your dancing shoes ...'

Those were the words whispered from heaven yesterday. Quick yet with a gentle voice, they were unmistakable to my listening spirit. But – dancing shoes?! I wrote it down, and then promptly ignored it.

Maybe the wires from heaven to earth got crossed mid-stream due to an unscheduled ash cloud and this was actually intended for someone a bit more balletic than me.

So this morning when I glanced at what I had written, I reminded Him, 'Lord, I don't dance ...'

'Dance.'

Suddenly I saw in my spirit a little child twirling, laughing, giggling, unhindered, innocent and at peace. Oh ... *That* is what it means to dance.

Regardless of her surroundings, this child simply enjoyed the life of the moment.

'... David went down and brought up the ark of God from the house of Obed-Edom to the City of David with rejoicing ... David, wearing a linen ephod, danced before the LORD with all his might, while he and the entire house of Israel brought up the ark of the LORD with shouts and the sound of trumpets.'
(2 Sam. 6:12,14)

'As soon as the sound of your greeting reached my ears, the baby in my womb leaped for joy.' (Luke 1:44)

David dances because he is watching the ark, which symbolises God's throne and presence, coming to rest in his city. John the Baptist, still a growing infant in his mother's womb, apparently leaps for joy when Jesus, also a growing infant in his mother's womb, enters the house. I love to imagine that – two unborn children dancing in their respective wombs, *simply because GOD was in the house.*

Let the Spirit of God release rhythm in your spirit today. Listen to the heartbeat of heaven and let loose a sound of praise over your home. Move in the unforced rhythms of grace, freely choosing His blessings whilst freely giving Him your burdens.

His presence will be your partner and the praises of heaven your music.

I double dare you ... DANCE!

Imagine yourself dancing as a young girl; dancing free, laughing, twirling, holding onto the hands of Jesus as He spins you around, loving life – let yourself enjoy this scene for a few minutes then pray a prayer of thanksgiving for LIFE!

Tuesday

'Il do it myself!' are words often muttered by young children learning to assert their independence. It is healthy and it is right, though at the same time it is often frustrating for the parent waiting for the task to be completed! Yet over time as we continue to assert our independence, we often make choices which have anything but positive effects on our lives. And these choices lead to burdens we then carry with us throughout our lives.

What are your greatest 'burdens' at the moment?

. . . .

. . . .

. . . .

. . . .

What keeps you from releasing those burdens to the Lord and trusting Him to carry them for you?

. . . .

. . . .

. . . .

. . . .

. . . .

Are there any areas in life where in essence
you have been saying to God 'I'll do it myself!'?
How is that working for you?

....

....

....

....

....

Lord, I have carried these burdens for longer than I care to
remember, and longer than has been necessary. I repent
of not trusting You with them and I ask for Your help in
releasing them to Your care. These burdens have become
unnecessary friends who have joined my path of life and
I would like them to leave. Please remove them from my
shoulders and Holy Spirit please convict me when I try to
welcome them back. Empower me, Lord, to walk free of
what You died to free me from. Amen.

Wednesday

Burdens come in many forms: concerns for other people, responsibilities at work, issues relating to health or finances. One by one and little by little these pressures are placed upon our shoulders and the thought of living light and free seems a childhood away.

But is this how Jesus wants us to live? Is this the freedom He died to bring us? Is there a better way?

Matthew 11:28–30 says, 'Come to me, all you who are weary and burdened, and I will give you rest. Take my yoke upon you and learn from me, for I am gentle and humble in heart, and you will find rest for your souls. For *my yoke is easy and my burden is light*' (emphasis mine). When we are yoked together with Christ, the road is not always easy, but with Him at our side, the burden then becomes light because He takes the weight of it.

What does it mean to you when Jesus says His yoke is easy and His burden is light?

....
....
....
....

If you are yoked together with Him (as oxen are yoked together when they plough a field) and He is taking the burden, then what is left for you to do? How does this make you feel?

....
....
....
....
....

How do we release our burdens to the Lord, yet also continue in compassion and prayer for other people? How did Jesus do this and what can we learn from Him?

....
....
....
....
....

Thursday

O ften we can feel irresponsible if we do *not* feel weighed down and burdened by something, as if we were not caring enough about our lives or the lives of others! Especially as women, there is a sense of needing to control our environment, and a maternal instinct which desires to remove the pain which others might be experiencing. In a strange way we feel neglectful if we are not worrying about a person or situation. Yet this is simply a lie of the enemy to hold us back from being all Christ wants us to be.

Would you agree that you tend to feel something is wrong if you are not worrying about something or someone? Why do you think this is?

....

....

....

In what areas of life do you find it most difficult to release control? Why is that?

....

....

....

....

Corrie ten Boom said, 'Worry does not empty
tomorrow of its sorrow; it empties today of its
strength'. Have you found that to be true in
your own life at all? Has there been a time when
you released your worry and burden to the
Lord, and found freedom and peace in the midst
of a difficult season?

. . . .

. . . .

. . . .

. . . .

. . . .

Spend some time praising God, thanking God
and worshipping God. Focusing on praise and
thanksgiving is one critical way of overcoming
worry and anxiety. If it's helpful, write out some
things you are thankful for and reasons why
today He is MOST worthy of your praise!

. . . .

. . . .

. . . .

. . . .

. . . .

Friday

The key is definitely found in choosing to be yoked together with Him, trusting Him and following His lead. It is also choosing to release our burdens onto His shoulders, not trying to carry them at the same time. He is big enough to carry the burden; He does not need our assistance. And finally, praise, thanksgiving and worship release us from focusing on the problems giving us space to embrace the presence – it is a great exchange!

Today imagine yourself yoked up with Christ – surrendered to His will for your life, knowing that He is good and His plans for you are good. Then imagine yourself releasing your burdens at the cross, and walking away from them in the freedom and empowerment of the Holy Spirit within you.

It is in this place, we are free to dance …

Today write a love letter to the Lord! Express

your adoration for Him, share what you love the

most about Him, tell Him how He makes you

feel and why you love His presence. And if this

seems foreign or difficult for you to do, then

possibly start by writing to Him your desire for

a greater closeness and understanding of His

character of love. Ask Him to reveal Himself to

you in special ways – share your heart with Him

... and don't forget, if you feel so inclined, to do

a little dance ...!

Monday

An Olives Convert

FREE *TO* INFLUENCE

'Be wise in the way you act towards
outsiders; make the most of every
opportunity.'(Col. 4:5)

Hi, my name is Jen and I am an olives convert.

For years I have hated olives. Not mildly disliked
– hated. I could not stand the taste, smell, look or
thought of eating an olive. I once strolled through an
olive grove in Israel enjoying the thought that Jesus
may have walked the same ground, but repulsed at the
notion of enjoying the same 'grub'!

Yet suddenly, seemingly overnight, I have converted
and even now as I type, an open jar of olives sits beside
me. What happened?

Influence.

I have a friend who loves his olives. When we are
out for an evening, his wife and I generally share the
cheese board, but Phil – he's an olive man. And from
our very first dinner he has been encouraging me to
try the olives, assuring me that over time I would come
to appreciate their unique qualities. I didn't believe
him, yet out of politeness would try to force one or two
down my throat before the urge to choke was just too

much. This continued for a long time until one day I noticed the repulsion level shifting. Why?

Influence.

Observing Phil gaining such pleasure from a simple bowl of olives only increased my desire to understand this elusive enjoyment. So I would try again, and each time they would get slightly easier to swallow. Until one day, much to the surprise of my taste buds, I ordered a bowl of olives purely for my own personal enjoyment.

Though it wasn't intentional, Phil had slowly influenced me over months of watching and listening to him, until I felt compelled to experience the same joy that he did.

That is the power of influence. *It draws in the doubter, until the doubter becomes the doer.*

In Christ, we have the power and ability to influence this world for His kingdom. People should be drawn to a joy we carry which they do not experience; their spiritual taste buds searching for the pleasure we find in the presence of the King.

Today, influence on purpose. Influence with
intentionality. Influence for results.

Because something far more rewarding than personal
taste is on the menu!

Do you find it easy to share your faith?
Are you intentionally influencing others
for the kingdom? How? How do you most
like to be influenced?

Tuesday

Over the course of these twelve weeks together, we have been enjoying a journey from various hindrances such as anxiety, sin, unforgiveness, fear, and regret, into a place of freedom. In this last devotional I want us to change the order and this time explore our freedom in *to* something: influence.

Often our Christian lives revolve around improvement. We work towards becoming 'better Christians', hoping that each passing year shows us a bit more Christlike and less self-centred than the previous one. Preachers are continually challenging us to let go of the sin which hinders us and instead move forward into the freedom which was bought for us on the cross. And that is both necessary and true!

Yet it is quite easy to get so caught up in improving, that we forget about influencing. If we are constantly improving, there is the subtle danger of 'waiting until I'm ready'; and if we do that, *the enemy will always convince us we are not ready.*

How would you define influence, when it comes to Christianity and kingdom living?

....

....

How comfortable do you feel influencing others for Christ (verbally, by praying, sharing your faith, doing acts of kindness, serving, etc)? What are the ways you typically influence?

....

....

Have you ever thought to yourself that once you were 'more ready', *then* you would evangelise or share your faith more? God can use us where we are at today – ask Him now if there is anyone He would like you to begin influencing on purpose?

Spend a few minutes praying for courage and boldness. Ask the Lord to give you a spirit of wisdom and understanding to know Him better (Eph. 1:17), then ask for direction on where and how to share this love with others. Write down any ideas He gives you in prayer.

Wednesday

Procrastination has been the demise of productivity for years. We put off what we can do today, hoping that it won't be necessary to do it tomorrow. *And the more we postpone, the less we produce.* In some areas of life this does not affect anyone but ourselves; but in the area of kingdom influence, procrastination is selfish.

If we have the ability to change someone else's life for good, and we choose not to, that is selfish behaviour. I realise for many of us fear is at the forefront as well, but even in that we are selfishly choosing to put our comfort zone above the opportunity of bringing blessing to someone else. May I pause here and interject – *I am speaking to myself!* So please do not be under any illusions that I am criticising you for something I am adept at, I am not.

I don't want my fear to become an excuse which hinders the release of God's favour. He wants to favour people, to bless the hurting, to heal the sick, to free those who are bound, and to use me (and you) to do this!

What are your greatest fears when it comes
to practically sharing the love of Christ with
someone?

....

....

....

What are one or two of your greatest
experiences/memories of practically sharing the
love of Christ with someone?

....

....

How do you feel about the fact that God wants
to use you to pray for the sick, encourage the
desperate, and witness to the wanderer?

....

....

....

Is there someone right now that you know God
wants you to influence and if so, who?

....

....

....

Thursday

Knowing that the Creator of the universe wants to
work in partnership with us is quite humbling, to
say the least! God could have made everyone a robot
with a set programme of what to do or forced us to
follow Him and His ways, but that is not His manner.
Instead, He gives us free will and encourages us to
make, for ourselves, the best choices for our lives.

The Bible says, 'How beautiful are the feet of those who
bring good news' (Rom. 10:15). (As one girl who has
never liked her feet, this verse has always brought me
encouragement!)

Another way to say this – *you carry something.*

**In what way do others know that you are
carrying 'good news' with you? Is it obvious?**

When carrying something we usually look for a place
to eventually lay the item down. Because as God's
children, the Holy Spirit lives *in* us, we carry with us the
presence of God, and it was never meant to be kept to
ourselves.

In what ways can we leave traces of that presence wherever we go?

....
....
....

Jesus says in Matthew 11:28–30 that we can take His yoke upon us because His burden is light and His yoke easy.

Are there any burdens you are carrying which need to be replaced by the peace of His presence instead?

....
....
....
....

Who has influenced you the most? In what way? How can you learn from their example in the way that you influence others?

....
....
....
....

Friday

You made it! Well done on reaching the final day of this devotional. You now have a treasure box of recorded thoughts and experiences to take with you into the next season; a season even more freedom-based than before!

On this final day I would like you to take time to review the past three months and some of the thoughts you have written, or words spoken by the Lord, as you have taken time out to be with Him. Have a quick glance back at some of your answers to the written questions.

What are one or two specific areas in which you would say you have grown the most? (Maybe simply doing a daily devotional is new to you?)

What has been the biggest challenge of the past few months as you have worked through these different themes? Which one was the most difficult for you and why?

After He was baptised, Jesus came out of the water and heard the following words: '… This is my Son, whom I love; with him I am well pleased' (Matt. 3:17). The Father gave His approval before Jesus had accomplished any ministry. In other words, *it was not about the performance, it was about the person.* Father God loves you as much as He loves His Son, because He *is* love. And it is not based on your performance or level of spirituality; He simply loves you because you are His creation.

Hear Him say to you 'well done'. Well done for persevering. Well done for studying and seeking more. Well done for being honest. Well done for resting in His grace. Well done good and faithful servant, *well done daughter*!

Use these last few minutes to pray that what God has shown you and what He has done in you over these last weeks will remain, making your future greater than your past!

If you prefer, a prayer is written out below for you to use as a guide:

Father, I thank You for everything You have shown me these past weeks. Thank You for Your kindness, goodness and grace toward me. I receive Your tangible love and comfort right now. Let this be the beginning of another chapter in my life, a fresh new season that we can walk through together. I declare the BEST is yet to come in my life and that my latter days will be greater than my former days! In Your name and to Your glory, Lord, Amen!

Inspiring Women Every Day
Daily Devotional

This bimonthly devotional is written by women, for women to inspire and encourage all ages.

• Increase your faith and ignite your passion for Jesus
• Find practical support to face life's challenges
• Be enlightened by insights into God's Word.

For current prices of our annual subscriptions or individual issues please visit our Online Store at **www.cwr.org.uk/store** Also available by daily email, eBook and Kindle.

For more information on *Inspiring Women Every Day* and other CWR publications please visit **www.cwr.org.uk**

Group Resources for Women

This dynamic new study combines biblical teaching with practical insights to encourage women all around the world to realise their potential and fight for the rights of their sisters in less fortunate circumstances. Readers are challenged not just to get angry or upset about statistics and situations but to turn emotion into action. A great resource for churches or small groups.

Because They're Worth It
by Amanda Jackson
978-1-85345-913-9
48 page paperback
210 x 148mm

Other group resources for women:

Seasons
978-1-85345-605-3

Designed for Living
978-1-85345-523-0

How to be a Secure Woman
978-1-85345-307-6

For current prices and more information please visit our website at **www.cwr.org.uk**

Courses and seminars

Publishing and new media

Conference facilities

Transforming lives

CWR's vision is to enable people to experience personal transformation through applying God's Word to their lives and relationships.

Our Bible-based training and resources help people around the world to:
• Grow in their walk with God
• Understand and apply Scripture to their lives
• Resource themselves and their church
• Develop pastoral care and counselling skills
• Train for leadership
• Strengthen relationships, marriage and family life and much more.

Our insightful writers provide daily Bible-reading notes and other resources for all ages, and our experienced course designers and presenters have gained an international reputation for excellence and effectiveness.

CWR's Training and Conference Centres in Surrey and East Sussex, England, provide excellent facilities in idyllic settings – ideal for both learning and spiritual refreshment.

 Applying God's Word
to everyday life and relationships

CWR, Waverley Abbey House,
Waverley Lane, Farnham,
Surrey GU9 8EP, UK

Telephone: **+44 (0)1252 784700**
Email: info@cwr.org.uk
Website: www.cwr.org.uk

Registered Charity No 294387
Company Registration No 1990308